Jazzicle Pops!

Ten jazzy, bluesy & funky songs for children

Trixi Field

includes: guidance notes, full score including guitar chords, lyric sheets for OHPs, separate recorder and piano parts

Also available separately: CD with sample performances and backings for all songs. For details please visit:
www.lulu.com/trixifield

Second edition

Voice Confidence Publications
www.trixifield.co.uk

Ten Jazzy, Bluesy & Funky Songs for Children

Jazzicle Pops!

Trixi Field

All rights reserved. *Except where specifically indicated*, no part of this book may be reproduced or transmitted in any form or by any means, electronic or mechanical, including photocopying or recording or by any information storage and retrieval system without permission from the author, except for the inclusion of brief quotations in a review.

Original copyright © 2003
This edition © 2008 by Trixi Field

ISBN 978-0-9559805-0-3

Cover design © 2008 Trixi Field
Cover photograph "Rock Singers" © 2008 Daniela Walter
(reproduced on the cover with the photographer's kind permission)

Contents

Introduction	3
General Notes	7
Lazy Tune	13
Notes	15
Full Score	17
CD track 1 (with voices) & 11 (accompaniment only)	
Mobile Phone Boogie	21
Notes	23
Full Score	26
CD track 2 (with voices) & 12 (accompaniment only)	
The Sleepover Song	35
Notes	37
Full Score	39
CD track 3 (with voices) & 13 (accompaniment only)	
Bumble Bee Calypso	45
Notes	47
Full Score	50
CD track 4 (with voices) & 14 (accompaniment only)	
How Can I Sing The Blues?	59
Notes	61
Full Score	64
CD track 5 (with voices) & 15 (accompaniment only)	
Hero's Lullaby	69
Notes	71
Full Score	73
CD track 6 (with voices) & 16 (accompaniment only)	
Song Train	77
Notes	79
Full Score	82
CD track 7 (with voices) & 17 (accompaniment only)	
School Uniform Blues	87
Notes	89
Full Score	90
CD track 8 (with voices) & 18 (accompaniment only)	
In The Hush	97
Notes	99
Full Score	101
CD track 9 (with voices) & 19 (accompaniment only)	
I Can't Get My Aeroplane To Fly	111
Notes	113
Full Score	115
CD track 10 (with voices) & 20 (accompaniment only)	
Appendix I: Lyrics	119
Appendix II: Recorder parts	141
Appendix III: Piano part	165

Ten Jazzy, Bluesy & Funky Songs for Children

Introduction

Ten Jazzy, Bluesy & Funky Songs for Children

Introduction

This collection of children's songs sets out to provide children aged 8-11 with a new, colourful and challenging song repertoire to enjoy singing and to use as material for school performances.

The collection covers subjects that children are likely to have experience of – mobile phones, sleepovers, toys, insects, school and so forth - and draws on jazz, blues and other popular musical styles.

It encourages schools to utilise a whole range of musical talents available, from young children who enjoy singing and playing instruments to members of staff who may be talented pianists or guitarists.

Arrangements include fully written-out piano parts for the teacher or another pianist, and, for some of the songs guitar chords, which can be used together with the piano part, or as an independent accompaniment.

Recorder parts supplied separately can also be used for other concert-pitch instruments that pupils may be learning, and there are opportunities to include whatever percussion instruments are readily available.

Percussion rhythms are not written into the arrangements. Instead, one or two suggestions are given in the notes to each song.

Guitar chords are also given in some of the arrangements; some of these are very simple and could be played by beginners or others should be manageable for children who have been learning for a while. A tablature can be found in the notes that follow.

For performance purposes these songs are flexible enough to be in two or three vocal parts with an orchestra of melodic and percussion instruments.

Where there are not sufficient resources, numbers of singers or players, or where part-singing might still prove to be rather challenging, the songs can be just as effective if performed in unison with only piano or guitar accompaniment.

> A separate CD is also available comprising:
> - Tracks containing full arrangements of each of the songs. (Tracks 1-10)
> - Backing tracks containing piano part and sometimes recorder only, in case a pianist or guitarist is not available within the school. (Tracks 11-20)

General Notes

Ten Jazzy, Bluesy & Funky Songs for Children

General Notes

Song	Theme	Style	Key/ mode	Parts
1. Lazy Tune	Music	Blues waltz	G blues	2 parts
2. Mobile Phone Boogie	Mobile phones /communication	Boogie	D major	Unison & 2-parts
3. The Sleepover Song	Friends/ pesky little brothers / sleepovers	Funk	A major/ C major	2 parts
4. Bumble Bee Calypso	Nature / humour	Calypso	D major	Unison & 2-parts
5. How Can I Sing The Blues	Blues, humour	Blues	C penta-tonic	Unison
6. Hero's Lullaby	Dreaming	Waltz ballad	D dorian/ F dorian	2 parts
7. Song Train	Singing / being together	Gospel	C major	Unison
8. School Uniform Blues	Fashion/clothes	Blues	E blues F blues	2 parts,
9. In the hush	Nature/ sea/ dawn	Ballad	C major & D major	2 parts
10. I Can't Get My Aeroplane To Fly	Toys/ humour	Ragtime	C major	

Recorders or other Melodic instruments:
Any of the following could be used using the recorder parts: recorders, violins, clarinets, flutes, glockenspiels, xylophones & any other available instruments at concert pitch.

All the accompanying notes referring to recorders and recorder parts are also relevant for other melodic instruments.

Percussion:
All kinds of drums: djembe, tambours, hand drums, bass drums, congas; – any other available larger drums; smaller instruments – tambourines, bongos, woodblocks, claves, sleighbells, cowbells, triangles, finger cymbals, home-made instruments such as dried pulses in containers, or anything that makes an interesting sound when hit, shaken or pinged! Notes include suggested rhythms for two or three groups of instruments: 1) larger drums; 2) smaller drums/wood instruments 3) metal instruments, claves, shakers.

Piano:
Piano parts are notated in full. The piano part is also provided as an accompanying CD.

Guitar:

List of guitar chords per song:

Lazy Tune	G, G7, C7, D7
The Sleepover Song	A, A7, C
Mobile Phone Boogie	D, G, A7
How Can I Sing The Blues	C, F, G7, C7, A7, Dm
Hero's Lullaby	Dm, Am, Fm, Cm, Em
Bumble Bee Calypso	D, G, A7
In The Hush	C, A7, Dm7, G7, D, B7, Em

Guitar Tablature:

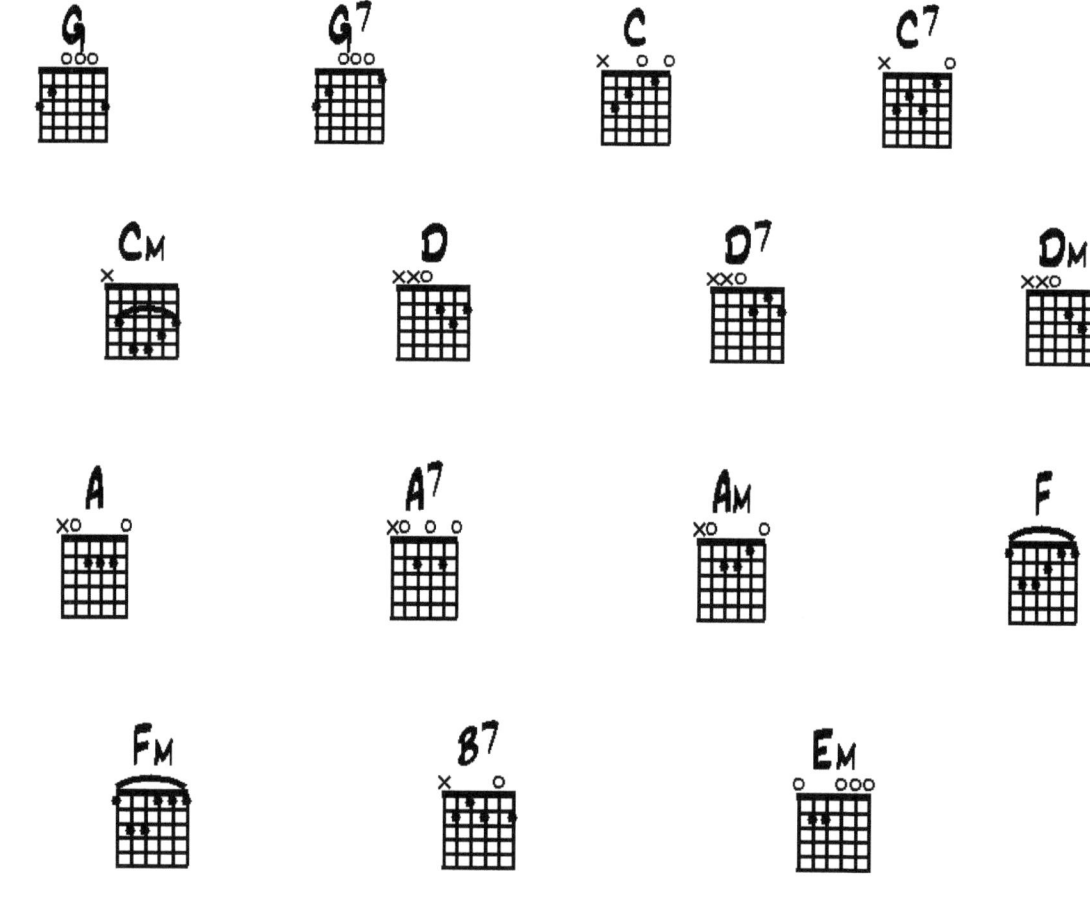

Vocal ranges per song (including all parts together):

Lazy Tune	Middle B to C (9th)
Mobile Phone Boogie	Middle D to A (5th)
Sleepover	Middle A to A (8ve)
Bumble Bee Calypso	Middle C# to D (9th)
How Can I Sing The Blues	Middle C to C (8ve)
Hero's Lullaby	Middle D to C (7th)
Song Train	Middle C to D (9th)
School Uniform Blues	Middle B to C (9th)
In the Hush	Middle B to B (8ve)
I Can't Get My Aeroplane To Fly	Middle B to A (7th)

Recorder (and/or other melodic instrument) notes required per song:

Performance

All songs can be performed exactly as arranged. However, suggestions are made in the notes to each song as to how singers, players and instruments can be used to create interesting contrasts in the performance of each song. These are not prescriptive, however, and with imagination and creative use of talents and resources available, many effective and exciting ways of presenting these songs could be found.

Lazy Tune

Lazy Tune

About the song

A laid-back, lullaby-like tune, as the title suggests. It is in waltz time, the rhythm suggesting the gentle rocking of a hammock, but the structure of the song is that of a blues.

The main body of the song consists of 12 bars using a simple blues melodic and harmonic structure, with a 3-line verse. There is a good deal of melodic repetition, making the song easy to learn.

Voices

Work on the tune first, line by line, pointing out to the singers the repetitions of the melody. Once the group can deliver the melody with confidence, encourage them to try to sing **mp** – as though they are trying to get a baby to sleep on a hammock. They might imagine that their voices are a soft breeze nudging the hammock to swing just enough to send the baby to sleep.

Part of the group could then take the lower, harmony line– this is very easy to learn as it consists mainly of repeated notes. Ensure that each group is solid and confident before putting the two parts together.

Recorders

Where recorders are indicated or mentioned, assume throughout the collection that this refers also to any other available instrument at concert pitch.

The recorder parts can be played by young players/beginners who have learnt the notes indicated in the general notes.

There are no difficult rhythms and children who have learned dotted minims (dotted half notes) and tied notes should be able to play this with little difficulty. Add the recorders to the voices after both have been thoroughly learned separately.

Guitar

Easy guitar chords:

  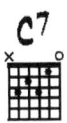 

Suggested percussion part:

If percussion is used in this piece, the emphasis should be on very gentle support. For example, instead of hitting a drum, the surface could be rubbed with a brush or fingertips, taking 3 beats to cover the circumference. A triangle could be added on the first beat of every other bar. For example:

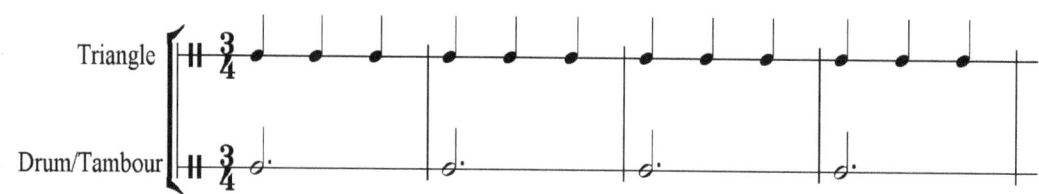

- where ♩. represents the movement of the brush or fingertips swishing once round the circumference of the drum. The above four bars would represent 4 'rounds' of the drum's circumference.

Performance

Since this is a short song it could be repeated two or three times, building up the texture with each repetition. For example:

Intro:	piano, guitar, all melodic instruments (no percussion)
1st time:	voices (tune only, no harmony), piano and/or guitar,
2nd time:	voices (2 parts), piano and/or guitar, soft percussion
3rd time:	voices (2 parts), piano, guitar, all melodic instruments, soft percussion
Coda:	piano, guitar, all melodic instruments (no percussion)

Experiment with different ensembles, either building the piece up, or starting with full orchestra and choir and building the piece down, or using soloists or small groups for a verse and so on, to find an arrangement that the group enjoys best for performance purposes.

Lazy Tune

Gently rocking, like a lullaby ♩ = 130

Music & Lyrics by Trixi Field

Copyright © 2000

Ten Jazzy, Bluesy & Funky Songs for Children

Mobile Phone Boogie

Ten Jazzy, Bluesy & Funky Songs for Children

Mobile Phone Boogie

About the song

A humorous and rumbustious song celebrating the noise and fun to be had with mobile phones. It has a simple A, B, A, B structure with two-part harmony in the B (chorus) sections. The style is boogie-woogie and the tempo is brisk and driving.

Voices

This is a fairly simple tune to learn, with plenty of repetition, but be aware of how the words cause variations in the rhythm of the tune.
- Spend some time working on diction – lyrics that are sung briskly need to be clearly enunciated if they are not to sound swallowed up.
- Chant the words in time before adding the tune to help achieve this.
- Note that some of the words are written in common abbreviated text mode, e.g. *"C U l8er"* (for "see you later"). *"XX"* can be pronounced *"ex ex"* or *"kiss kiss"*, whichever the children find easier to sing.
- Choruses: tackle each part separately, and ensure in both parts that the F#s and Fs are clearly differentiated.

Recorders

Relatively easy with mainly crotchets and semibreves. The only bar that may need special attention is the last in each introduction, where the last note anticipates the beat:

Guitar

Very easy; this part can be played by relative beginners.
The chords required are:

Suggested percussion part:

The following can be played quite vigorously to match the mood of the song, but it is important not to let the percussion sound overwhelm the singers.

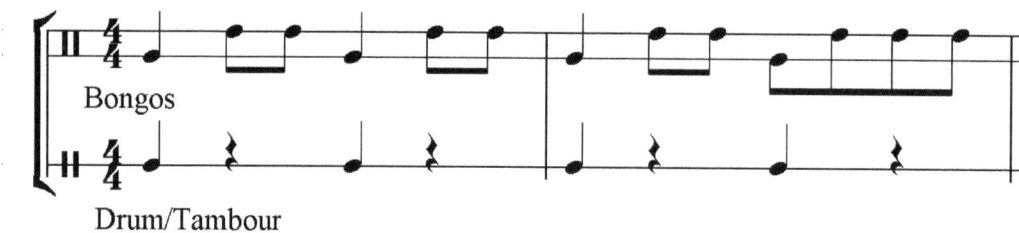

Other low and higher-pitched instruments can be used, depending upon the resources available.

Suggested last bar of the coda:

Performance

To achieve a fun and lively performance, try the following

arrangement:

Intro: voices, piano, 3-4 guitars, recorders only
Verse 1: voices, piano, guitars
Chorus 1: guitars, recorders only
Intro, verse 2 and chorus 2: voices, piano, guitars, recorders and other melodic
Instruments, percussion group.

Although energy and drive are important qualities in this song, be careful not to allow the orchestration to swamp the words.

Ten Jazzy, Bluesy & Funky Songs for Children

Mobile Phone Boogie

Music & Lyrics by Trixi Field

Ten Jazzy, Bluesy & Funky Songs for Children

Jazzicle Pops!

Ten Jazzy, Bluesy & Funky Songs for Children

Jazzicle Pops!

33

The Sleepover Song

Ten Jazzy, Bluesy & Funky Songs for Children

The Sleepover Song

About the song

A simple but energetic funky song about inviting friends round for a sleepover, and the practical jokes little brothers and their friends can get up to. It has a repeated ostinato riff in the piano, and very easy recorder and guitar parts. A good 'warm up' song.

Voices

- Work on the rhythm of the words first – the tune will be easy to add once the rhythm is strong and confident.
- Work on tune (top line) and then the harmony; once these are sung confidently, put them together.

The girls' names in the song could be substituted with names of members of the class.

Recorders

This part is very simple, based on A and C, allowing younger instrumentalists/beginners to be involved with the song. Practice clapping the rhythm, before getting the recorder group to play it.

Guitar

Very easy guitar part. Chords required are:

 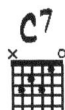

but if necessary, they can be substituted with:

Suggested percussion part:

Try a simple rhythm that complements the recorder rhythm, for example:

Performance

Since this is a very short song, there is little need to provide contrasts from verse to verse. It will work equally well simply arranged for voices and piano, with or without recorder, guitar and/or percussion.

The Sleepover Song

Bouncy & funky ♩= 140

Music & Lyrics by Trixi Field

Ten Jazzy, Bluesy & Funky Songs for Children

Jazzicle Pops!

Ten Jazzy, Bluesy & Funky Songs for Children

Jazzicle Pops!

Bumble Bee Calypso

Bumble Bee Calypso

About the song

A humorous song celebrating the humble bumble bee in a calypso style. It is up-tempo, with easy recorder and guitar parts. Piano and voices have some interesting and challenging calypso rhythms.

Voices

- Work through the rhythm of verse 1 by chanting the words line by line, to ensure that the rhythm and diction are clear and confident.
- Next, add the melody to the words.
- Once the group can sing verse 1 with confidence, move on to verses 2 and 3, chanting and then applying the melody in the same way.
- Chorus: chant through the words, to ensure that the rhythm is clear;
- work through each part separately, and then put the two parts together.

The group is now ready to put the whole song together.

Recorders

There two recorder parts in this song, but these are easy to play. The rhythm comprises mainly semi-breves, with one or two crotchets.

Piano

Watch out for cross rhythms – try to maintain left-hand rhythms, as these are an essential component of calypso.

Guitar

Very easy chords:

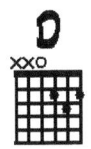   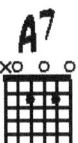

Suggested percussion part:

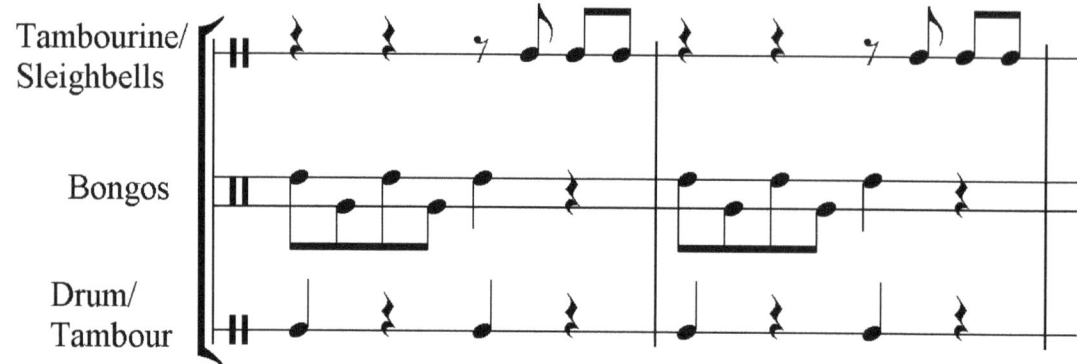

The texture is a little more complex than in earlier tunes. The percussion group can warm up by doing the following exercises:

Bongo group tap the rhythm on their knees and chant the words shown below:

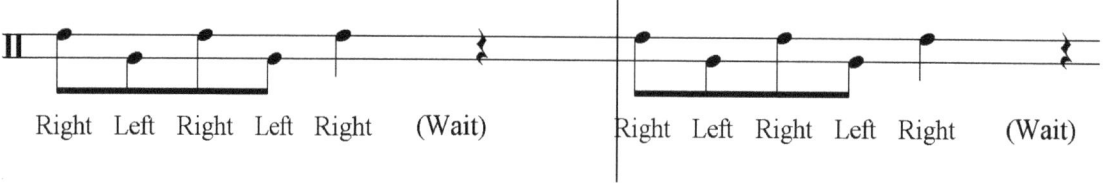

.Transfer the rhythm onto bongos or woodblocks, without saying "wait" (but still thinking them).

Tambourine group count and clap as follows:

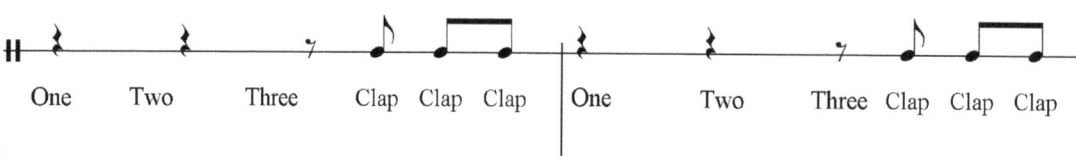

Transfer the rhythm onto tambourines or sleighbells without saying the words "clap clap clap" (but still thinking them)

Drums clap as follows:

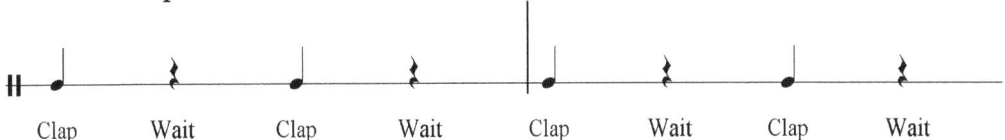

Put the two rhythms together at a time before the whole group plays together:
- tambour/drum & bongos
- tambour/drum & tambourine/sleighbells
- bongos & tambourine/sleighbells
- all three groups.

Performance

Here are two performance suggestions:
Intro: all instruments
Verse 1:   piano, voices
Chorus 1:   all instruments
Intro to v.2:   all instruments
Verse 2:   piano, voices
Chorus 2:   all instruments
Intro to v 3:   all instruments
Verse 3:   piano, voices
Chorus 3:   all instruments
Coda: all instruments

Intro: piano (left hand only), guitar, recorder, bongos
Verse 1:   piano (left hand only), guitar, voices
Chorus 1:   as intro, but piano plays both hands
Intro to v2:   piano (left hand only), guitar, recorders, bongos, tambourine
Verse 2:   piano (left hand only), guitar, voices, bongos
Chorus 2:   piano both hands, guitar, recorders, voices, bongos, tambourine
Intro to v3   all instruments
Verse 3   piano, guitar, voices, recorders, bongos, tambourines
Chorus 3:   all instruments
Coda: all instruments

Ten Jazzy, Bluesy & Funky Songs for Children

Bumble Bee Calypso

Music & Lyrics by Trixi Field

Jazzicle Pops!

Ten Jazzy, Bluesy & Funky Songs for Children

Jazzicle Pops!

55

Ten Jazzy, Bluesy & Funky Songs for Children

Ten Jazzy, Bluesy & Funky Songs for Children

How Can I Sing The Blues?

How Can I Sing The Blues?

About the song

A humorous song about the dilemma of the blues singer: to be a blues singer you have to be really miserable. The singers are upset because they are too happy to sing the blues! The song also tells us something about the blues: that it is normally a sad song.

It has a traditional blues structure, that is, a 3-line verse, 12 bars, and a standard blues harmonic progression. The tune is easy, based on a C pentatonic.

Notice that the groove is SWING. This means reading each pair of quavers:

as triplets:

so that the tune written thus:

1. You can sing the blues when the skies are dull and grey

actually sounds:

This becomes clear when listening to the CD recording.

Voices

- Work through the tune first.
- As usual, chanting the words in rhythm before adding the tune is a good way to start.
- At the end of each phrase there is a 7-beat pause for the singers. One way of ensuring the singers wait for the full 7 beats is to encourage them to clap the beats while they are chanting the words.

Guitar

Chords required:

Suggested percussion part:

Performance

Since the tune is repetitive, the song works well if the verses have contrasting arrangements. For example:

Intro:	Piano & percussion
Verse 1:	Girls, piano
Chorus:	All voices, piano, guitar & percussion
Verse 2:	Boys, piano
Chorus:	All voices, piano, guitar & percussion
Verse 3:	All voices, piano & guitar
Chorus:	All voices, piano, guitar & percussion

Hero's Lullaby

Ten Jazzy, Bluesy & Funky Songs for Children

Hero's Lullaby

About the song

A gentle song about dreaming based on D Dorian and F Dorian modes (with a fleeting visit to E Dorian). These minor-flavoured modes evoke an ethereal quality to the tune to suit the mood of the song.

As with "Lazy Tune", the waltz time suggests the rocking feel of a lullaby. And the melodic repetition helps to make this a relatively easy song to learn.

There is a very simple second part for voices consisting mainly of repeated notes, once again, not dissimilar to that of "Lazy Tune". This part is optional.

Voices

- Work through the tune first, line by line, (minus introduction and coda). Point out the repetitions of the melody to help singers pick up the patterns of the song more quickly.
- The song should be sung quietly to give the feeling of floating inside a wonderful dream.
- A group of the singers can then learn the second part, if desired.
- Once each group of voices can sing its part with confidence, put both together.
- Finally, work on the introduction and coda. These should be sung very gently – to help capture the mood the singers might try to imagine their sound as a soft warm cloud drifting into a child's bedroom, whispering the child into a deep, dreamy sleep.

Recorders

Very easy. Recorder players should also play quietly. You might suggest that they try to sound like guardian angels gently hovering above the sleeper.

Guitar

Relatively easy, but not necessarily for beginners:

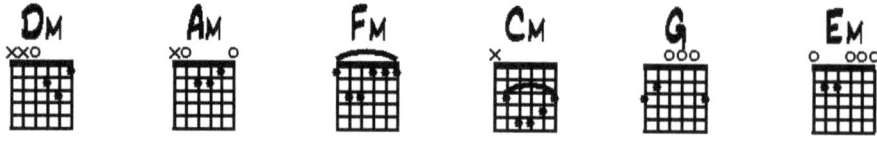

Suggested percussion part:

Keep this to a minimum – possibly only a triangle or soft cymbal:

Alternatively, try using the suggestions given for "Lazy Tune".

Performance

There are a number of ways the song could be interpreted. Here are a couple of suggestions:

Building the song up:

Intro:	recorders with piano
Verse 1:	voices I only with piano
Verse 2:	voices I, recorders, percussion and piano
Verse 3	voices I & II, recorders and/or any other melodic instruments, percussion, piano and guitar
Coda:	all instruments

ABA arrangement:

Intro:	all instruments with piano
Verse 1:	voices I & II with piano
Verse 2:	voices I & II with all instruments
Verse 3:	voices I & II with piano
Coda:	all instruments with piano

Hero's Lullaby

Ten Jazzy, Bluesy & Funky Songs for Children

Jazzicle Pops!

Song Train

Ten Jazzy, Bluesy & Funky Songs for Children

Song Train

About the song

This unison song is based on the 'train-to-heaven' kind of gospel/spiritual song.

It has a strong, repeated melodic and rhythmic shape making the song fairly easy to learn. However, it has a slightly unusual change of key and there is a range of a 9th in the melody. Because of this, it is probably better suited to older children, around age 10-11.

Voices

- Teach the tune of the first verse line by line.
- Notice that the melodic shape of line 2 is an echo of line 1, in F pentatonic.
- Line 3 is similar to line 1.
- Care needs to be taken over the rhythm, particularly anticipated beats as follows:

and

- Since such rhythms are commonplace in pop music, they shouldn't present too much difficulty, but it is as well to ensure they are sung accurately and with confidence.
- Chanting the rhythm of the words before learning the tune is often a useful way to work through challenging rhythms.
- You might like to spend extra time on the coda to achieve a crispness in the rhythm and the abrupt end, and to ensure the singers achieve clear contrasts in the dynamics as indicated in the coda.

Recorders

This part is very simple and allows younger instrumentalists/beginners to be involved with the song. Most of the rhythm is very straightforward.

Suggested percussion parts:

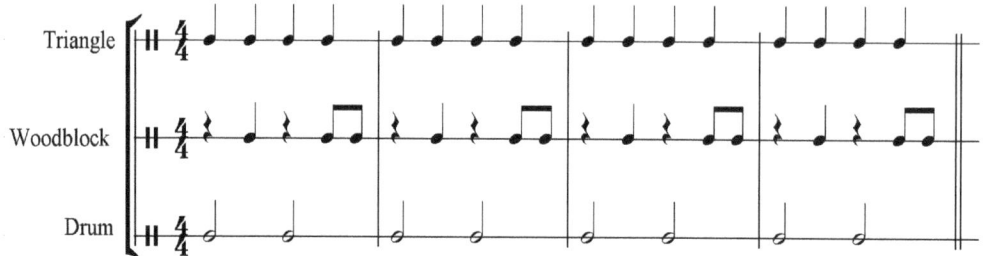

If the above ensemble proves too challenging, you might use simply the drum or triangle on their own.

Performance

Each of the three verses could involve different mixes of the instruments as accompaniments.

For example, building up verse by verse:

Intro: piano
Verse 1:   voices and piano
Verse 2:   voices, piano and melodic instruments
Verse 3:   voices, piano, melodic instruments, percussion and guitar
Coda: voices, all instruments.

Or: creating contrasts

Intro: piano
Verse 1:   all instruments, all voices
Verse 2:   small ensemble of voices and piano
Verse 3:   all instruments, all voices
Coda: all instruments, all voices

Ten Jazzy, Bluesy & Funky Songs for Children

Song Train

Music & Lyrics by Trixi Field

School Uniform Blues

School Uniform Blues

About the song

A humorous blues song, the tune & structure of which are relatively simple – a repeated melodic line with minimal variation, and standard blues harmony. There is a key change in the last verse. The song is in two parts, the lower part being the tune. The upper, harmony part is optional.

Voices

Although the tune is constant from verse to verse, there are rhythmic variations in the lyrics for each verse.
- Chant through the words of verse 1 to ensure clarity both in diction and in rhythm before adding the melody.
- Work similarly through verses 2, 3 and verse 4, all in the same key to begin with.
- Adding the harmony voice is optional, but go about it in the same way as the tune, and put the parts together when both can be sung with confidence
- Try out the key change on the last verse. Then put the whole song together, complete with introduction.

Recorders

Very easy.

Suggested percussion part:

Try fitting the percussion parts from "How Can I Sing The Blues" to this song, but without the swing groove.

Performance

This song already builds up verse by verse in the arrangement of the voices, from unison in verse 1 to 3 parts, recorders & melodic instruments and a key change in verse 4. You might use percussion to build the song up still further, and to create a "grand finale" in the final verse.

School Uniform Blues

Jolly, with an end-of-term feel! ♩ = 140

Music & Lyrics by Trixi Field

Jazzicle Pops!

Ten Jazzy, Bluesy & Funky Songs for Children

92

Jazzicle Pops!

Ten Jazzy, Bluesy & Funky Songs for Children

Jazzicle Pops!

Ten Jazzy, Bluesy & Funky Songs for Children

In The Hush

Ten Jazzy, Bluesy & Funky Songs for Children

In The Hush

About the song

A gentle two-part song about the sea and the dawn with a pop ballad feel to it. It has a simple A B structure, the B section closely resembling A. The song may be best suited to older children – around 10-11 years old. It will work well either as a unison song, or in two parts. There is a key change in verse 3

Recorders or other melodic instruments – violins may work well here - can be added in verse 3.

Voices

- Start with the tune for all voices, focusing on verse 1. Care needs to be taken over the rhythm of the words. It may be useful to start with chanting, as in earlier songs.
- Once singers can manage the melody and rhythm with confidence, add the second voice. Verses 2 and 3 should be easy once verse 1 is mastered.
- It may be wise to master the song with no key change to begin with.
- Once the singers can perform this with confidence, the key change can be introduced.

Dynamics are contrasting from verse to verse – encourage the singers to make as much contrast as possible, without losing the sweetness of tone required for this song. Smaller and larger groups of singers may be a way easily to achieve the dynamic contrasts

Recorders

These make their appearance in all introductions and verse 3, and would need to be played by older children who may have been learning their instrument for a while. Once the parts can be played with confidence, encourage contrasting dynamics.

Guitar

Rather more challenging. This is for young guitarists with more experience.
Chords are as follows:

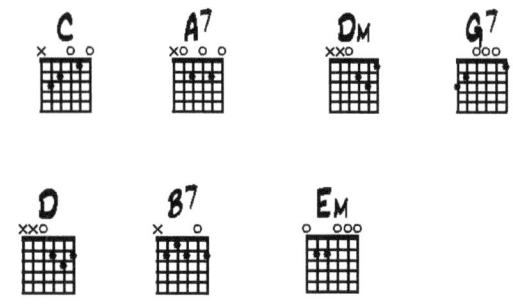

Performance

The song works well performed as written, but for a change, try using soloists or small ensembles for part of this song. For example:

Intro: piano, recorders
Verse 1:   solo (or small ensemble), tune only, piano
Verse 2:   duet (or small ensemble in two parts), piano
Verse 3:   whole group, piano, guitar, recorders

Jazzicle Pops!

In The Hush

Music & Lyrics by Trixi Field

1. In the hush of the morn - ing when the cur - tains are still

Ten Jazzy, Bluesy & Funky Songs for Children

Ten Jazzy, Bluesy & Funky Songs for Children

105

Ten Jazzy, Bluesy & Funky Songs for Children

Jazzicle Pops!

Ten Jazzy, Bluesy & Funky Songs for Children

I Can't Get My Aeroplane To Fly

I Can't Get My Aeroplane To Fly

About the song

A humorous song in a jaunty, ragtime style. The tune is fairly simple and unison, and there are three verses, making the song relatively easy to learn, although it should go at a fairly brisk pace.

Voices

- Start rehearsing relatively slowly: as before, encourage the group to chant the words to learn the rhythm with confidence.
- The tune is the same for every verse, but the words demand slightly different rhythms in places.
- Focus on each verse separately, with special attention given to the coda on verse 3.

Suggested percussion part:

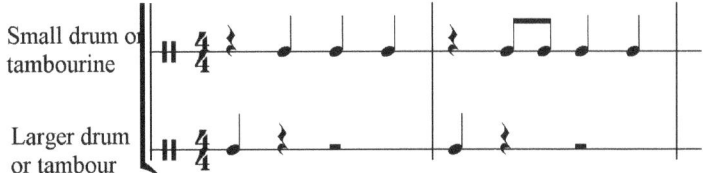

At the end of the introduction, and the end of each verse, the following rhythm could be used:

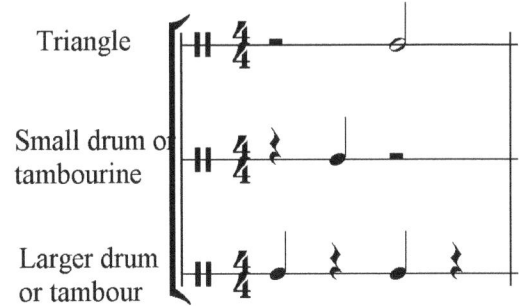

Performance

Here are some suggested arrangements:

Intro:	piano, percussion
Verse 1:	girls, piano
Verse 2:	boys, piano, quiet percussion
Verse 3:	all voices, piano, percussion
Coda:	all instruments

Intro:	all
Verse 1:	all
Verse 2:	small group of singers and piano
Verse 3:	all
Coda:	all

Jazzicle Pops!

I Can't Get My Aeroplane To Fly

Music & Lyrics by Trixi Field

Jazzicle Pops!

Ten Jazzy, Bluesy & Funky Songs for Children

Appendix I

Lyrics

Can be photocopied onto acetate for OHPs

1. Lazy Tune

It's a mellow, lazy tune

Like a hazy afternoon

Voices sighing, voices low,

Lullabying, swinging, slow

It's a mellow, lazy tune

Like the soft and gentle moon.

2. Mobile Phone Boogie

Verse 1

When I'm upstairs in my room or up in a tree

I'll start in the morning and keep going till three

I'll do it in a bus and then I'll talk really loud

In a car, in a train or in the middle of a crowd

On my own, in a cave or down in a crater

I'll text you a message saying "C U L8er"!

Chorus 1

C U l8er, I'll C U l8er,

C U l8er, I'll C U l8er,

C U l8er, I'll C U l8er,

C U l8er, I'll C U l8er,

On my own, in a cave or down in a crater

I'll text you a message saying "C U L8er"!

Verse 2

I often like to start the day by texting a friend

Say "Hi" and " Howzit going XX" then press send

I'm never feeling lonely, no, I'm never alone

When I call my best friend on my mobile phone

I love to send a message or a text 2 U

Even though I'm sitting here right next 2 U.

Chorus 2

Next 2 U, right next 2 U,

next 2 U, right next 2 U

Next 2 U, right next 2 U,

next 2 U, right next 2 U

I love to send a message or a text 2 U

Even though I'm sitting here right next 2 U.

3. The Sleepover Song

Verse 1

Girls:

Emma and Jane and Nita are coming to sleep over tonight

We'll talk and eat and laugh and joke, and then we'll have a pillow fight

Tired in the morning, 'cos we won't sleep till one

It'll be fun.

Verse 2

Boys:

My sister and her schoolfriends are having a sleepover tonight

We'll put beetles in the sheets and bugs in the bed, and give them a massive fright

Girls:

Aaaargh!

Boys:

Tired in the morning, they'll fall asleep at school

It'll be cool

Girls:

Cool! Cool! Cool! Cool!

All:

Cool! Cool! Cool! Cool!

Cool!

4. Bumble Bee Calypso

Verse 1

I love summer but I hate the wasps

And I don't think the wasps like me

If I have to have a bug land on my nose

I'd rather it was a bumble bee

Chorus

'Cos the bumble bee is a teddy bear

He's big and fat and round

Yes, the bumble bee is all covered in hair

He's funny and fuzzy with a bizzy buzzy sound.

Verse 2

The bumble bee is a cute little buggle

He's jolly and round and fat

If I were so small I would give him a huggle

But I can't, or else I'll squash him flat

Chorus

'Cos the bumble bee is a teddy bear

He's big and fat and round

Yes, the bumble bee is all covered in hair

He's funny and fuzzy with a bizzy buzzy sound.

Verse 3

He may not be stripey, he may not be yellow

But if a bumble you should spy

Spare a little thought for this jolly woolly fellow

He may be a little lump but he can fly

Chorus

'Cos the bumble bee is a teddy bear

He's big and fat and round

Yes, the bumble bee is all covered in hair

He's funny and fuzzy with a bizzy buzzy sound.

5. How Can I Sing The Blues

Verse 1

You can sing the blues when the skies are dull and grey

You can sing the blues if you've had a horrid day

You can sing the blues if you can't go out to play

Chorus

I'm sad 'cos I'm happy and that just doesn't do,

If you're happy and you sing the blues, it won't sound true

So how can I sing the blues if I ain't blue?

Verse 2

You can sing the blues if you're feeling down and out,

If you're lonely, angry, sad or full of doubt,

'Cos feeling sad is what the blues is all about

Chorus

I'm sad 'cos I'm happy and that just doesn't do,

If you're happy and you sing the blues, it won't sound true

So how can I sing the blues if I ain't blue

Verse 3

If you want to sing the blues you can't feel good,

I would sing about my sadness if I could,

But I don't feel half as rotten as I should

Chorus

I'm sad 'cos I'm happy and that just doesn't do,

If you're happy and you sing the blues, it won't sound true

So how can I sing the blues if I ain't blue

6. Hero's Lullaby

Verse 1

Here in my dreams I dive into the deep, ah, ah,

Being the hero whenever I sleep, ah, ah,

Saving a damsel or catching a thief

Floating to earth like a leaf

Until my clock starts to bleep, and ends my deep sleep.

Verse 2

Here in my slumber I'm no longer me, ah, ah

Being what I've always wanted to be, ah, ah

Dolphin or butterfly, lion or mare,

Doing what I'd never dare,

Till my mum brings me some tea, and gently wakes me

Verse 3

Wish I could stay and dream on through the day, ah, ah

Winter no more, just a long sunny May, ah, ah

Gliding or diving or being a star,

Driving a shiny red car

Till the sun's first golden ray brings a new day

Ah, ah, ah, ah.

7. Song Train

Verse 1

Come and join us here on the song train

We've got lots of room because it's a long train

We can give so much love to make it a strong chain

We'll roll all over the world singing our song, chugging along

Come on and join the song

Verse 2

Come and join us here on the song boat

There are lots of people here on our long boat

We can ride all the waves because it's a strong boat

We'll roll all over the world singing our song, sailing along

Come on and join the song

Verse 3

Come and join us here on the song plane

If you want to fly, don't get on the wrong plane,

We can weather the storm because it's a strong plane

We'll fly all over the world singing our song, soaring along

Come on and join the

Come on and join the

Come on and join the song!

8. School Uniform Blues

Verse 1

I've got to wear my uniform when I go to school

I've got to wear my uniform when I go to school

But when the weekend comes and I'm home, well I look cool.

Verse 2

I've got some wicked jeans and a crazy pair of shoes

I've got some wicked jeans and a crazy pair of shoes

But then on Monday morning I get the school uniform blues.

Verse 3

Well I can't wait for the summer when there's no more black and grey

Well I can't wait for the summer when there's no more black and grey

Gonna wear green and orange and red and blue ev'ry day

Verse 4

Gonna wear lots of colour and dress just like the sun

Gonna wear lots of colour and dress just like the sun

Gonna be no more uniform, gonna have me some fun!

Oh yeah!

9. In The Hush

Verse 1

In the hush of the morning, when the curtains are still drawn

We'll steal away to the edge of the seashore, to watch the glow of the dawn.

In the silence just before sunrise, not a soul in sight

We'll watch the day unfolding, taking leave of the night.

Verse 2

When the day is a-dawning, and the birds wake from their rest,

We'll steal away just to watch the horizon, to see the sky at her best.

As the gulls start crying "it's morning!" we'll go back to bed

And we'll pretend we stayed home, busy sleeping instead.

Verse 3

When the raindrops are falling, and the day is dull and long,

Then we'll remember the edge of the seashore and the early seagull's song.

When I'm sad, when I'm lonely, not a friend in sight,

Then I'll remember the seashore, and the dawn's gentle light.

10. I Can't Get My Aeroplane To Fly

Verse 1

No matter how I try,

I can't get my aeroplane to fly

I've stuck a lot of bits on it

And a plastic pilot who sits on it

But however much I try,

I can't get my aeroplane to fly.

Verse 2

However hard I throw,

I can't get my aeroplane to go

I've tried adding extra wings

And other funny little whirly things

But no matter how I throw,

I can't get my aeroplane to go.

Verse 3

So even though I've tried,

My aeroplane won't glide

I've turned it into a little car

But still it won't go very far

And although I've tried and tried

It looks as though it died

'Cos it's landed on its side

And my aeroplane won't glide.

Appendix II

Recorder parts

Can be photocopied as required

Jazzicle Pops!

Descant Recorder I

Lazy Tune

Gently rocking, like a lullaby ♩ = 130

Music & Lyrics by Trixi Field

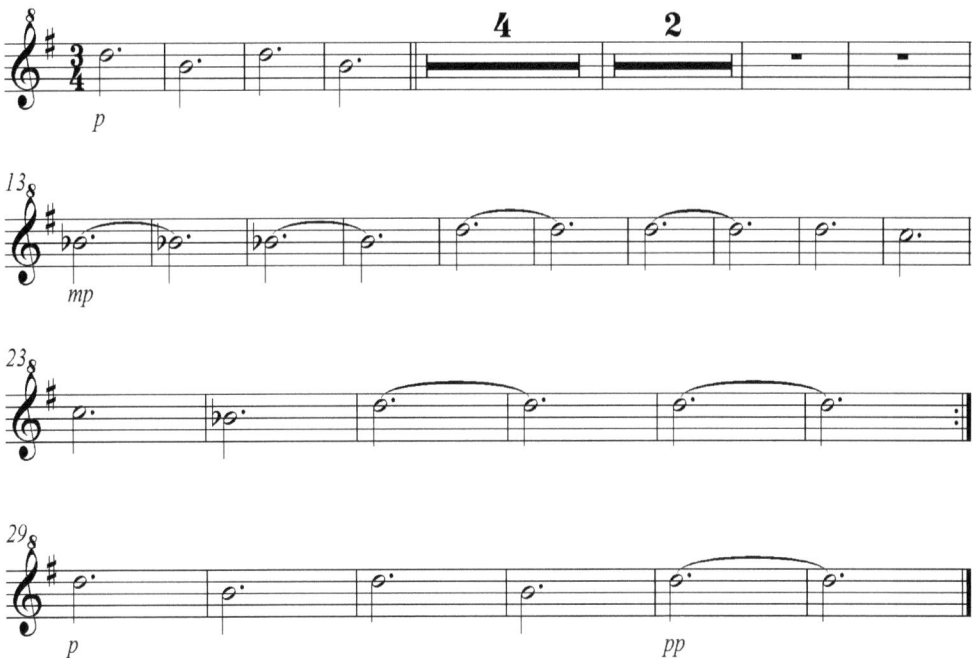

Ten Jazzy, Bluesy & Funky Songs for Children

Descant Recorder II

Lazy Tune

Gently rocking, like a lullaby ♩ = 130

Music & Lyrics by Trixi Field

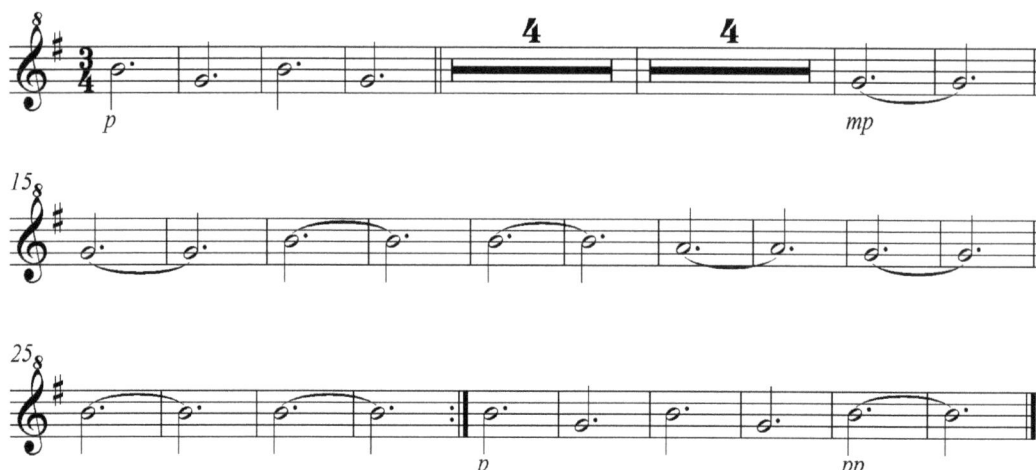

Descant Recorder III

Lazy Tune

Gently rocking, like a lullaby ♩ = 130

Music & Lyrics by Trixi Field

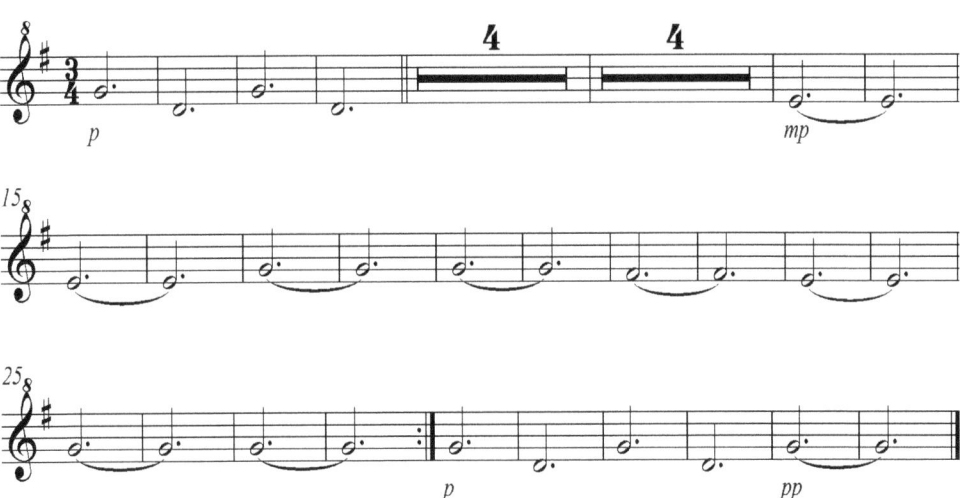

Ten Jazzy, Bluesy & Funky Songs for Children

Descant Recorder I, page 1 of 3

Mobile Phone Boogie

Music & Lyrics by Trixi Field

Driving and Rumbustuous ♩ = 130

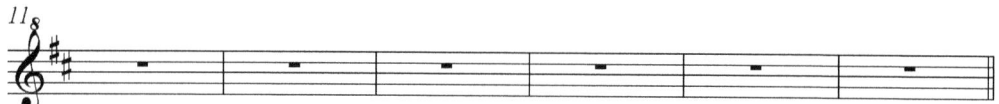

Mobile Phone Boogie: Descant Recorder I, page 2 of 3

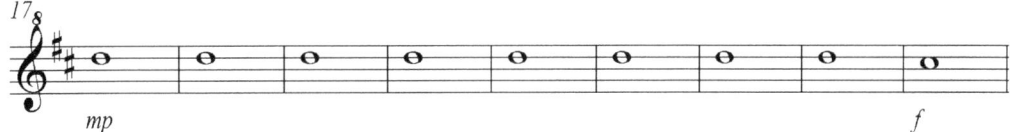

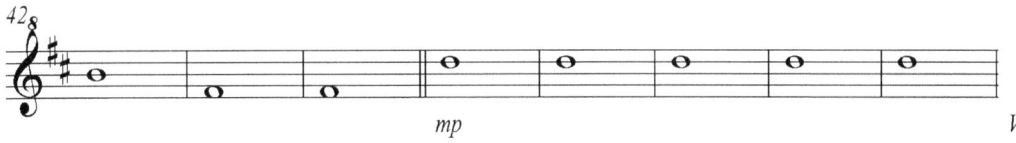

Mobile Phone Boogie: Descant Recorder I, page 3 of 3

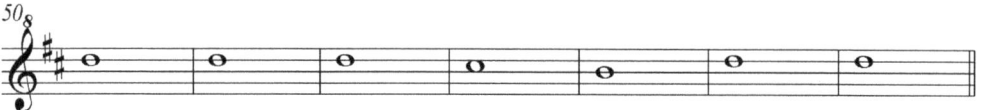

Descant Recorder II, page 1 of 3

Mobile Phone Boogie

Driving and Rumbustuous ♩ = 130

Music & Lyrics
by Trixi Field

Mobile Phone Boogie: Descant Recorder II, page 2 of 3

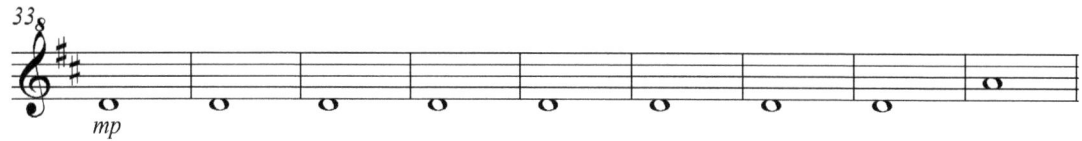

Mobile Phone Boogie: Descant Recorder II, page 3 of 3

Ten Jazzy, Bluesy & Funky Songs for Children

Descant Recorder

The Sleepover Song

Bouncy & funky ♩ = 140

Music & Lyrics by Trixi Field

Bumble Bee Calypso: Descant Recorder I, page 2 of 2

Descant Recorder II, page 1 of 2

Bumble Bee Calypso

Music & Lyrics by Trixi Field

Bumble Bee Calypso: Descant Recorder II, page 2 of 2

Descant Recorder

Hero's Lullaby

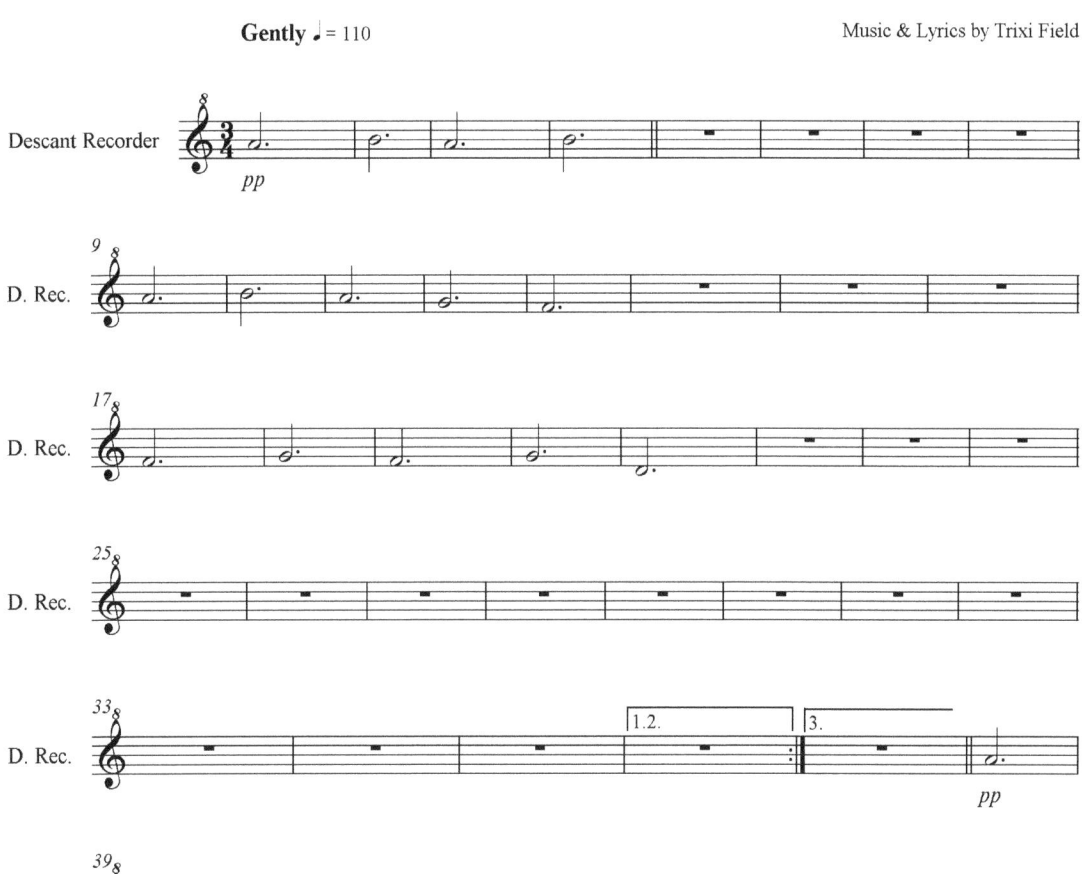

Ten Jazzy, Bluesy & Funky Songs for Children

Descant Recorder

Song Train

Music & Lyrics by Trixi Field

Descant Recorder I

School Uniform Blues

Jolly, with an end-of-term feel! ♩ = 140

Music & Lyrics by Trixi Field

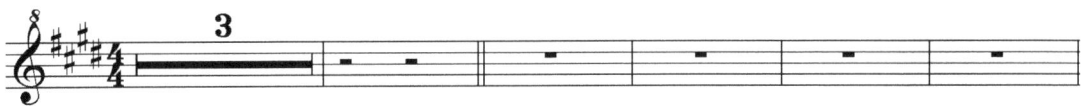

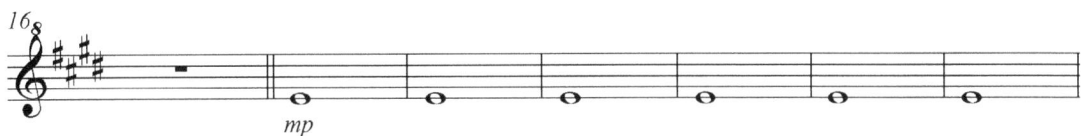

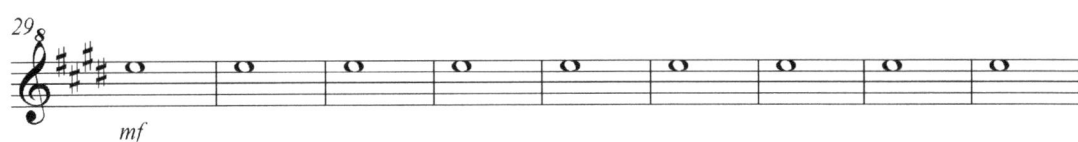

Ten Jazzy, Bluesy & Funky Songs for Children

Descant Recorder II

School Uniform Blues

Jolly, with an end-of-term feel! ♩ = 140

Music & Lyrics by Trixi Field

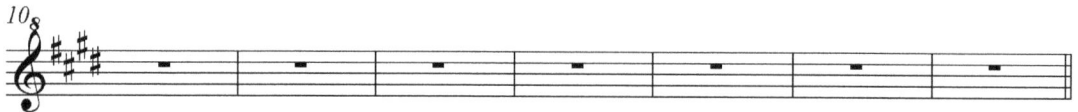

Descant Recorder I, page 1 of 2

In The Hush

Music & Lyrics by Trixi Field

Descant Recorder II, page 1 of 2

In The Hush

Music & Lyrics by Trixi Field

Gentle ♩ = 100

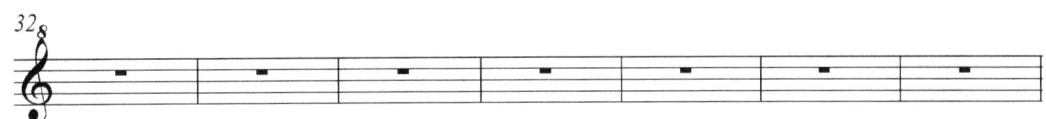
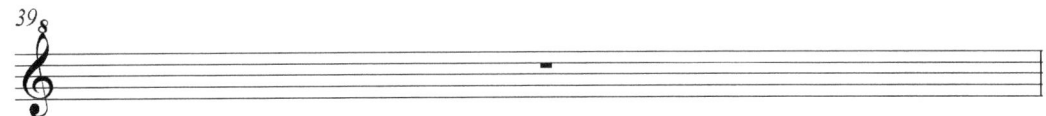

In The Hush: Descant Recorder II, page 2 of 2

Appendix III

Piano part

Can be photocopied once

Lazy Tune

Gently rocking, like a lullaby ♩ = 130

Music & Lyrics by Trixi Field

Lazy Tune: Piano page 2 of 2

Ten Jazzy, Bluesy & Funky Songs for Children

Mobile Phone Boogie

Driving and Rumbustuous ♩ = 130

Music & Lyrics
by Trixi Field

V.S.

Mobile Phone Boogie: Piano page 2 of 5

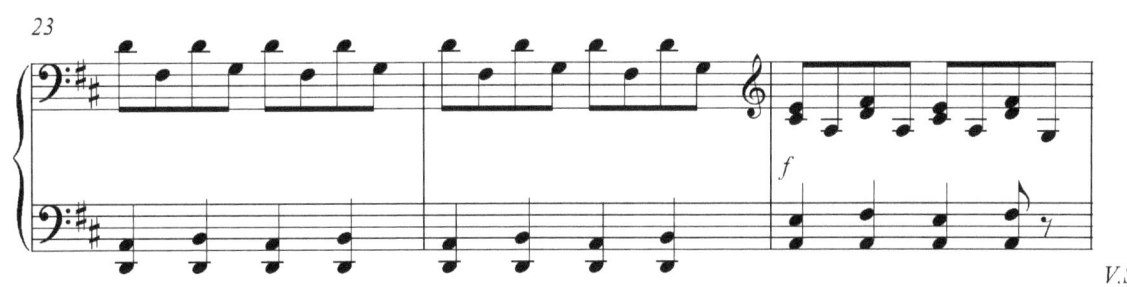

Mobile Phone Boogie: Piano page 3 of 5

Mobile Phone Boogie: Piano page 4 of 5

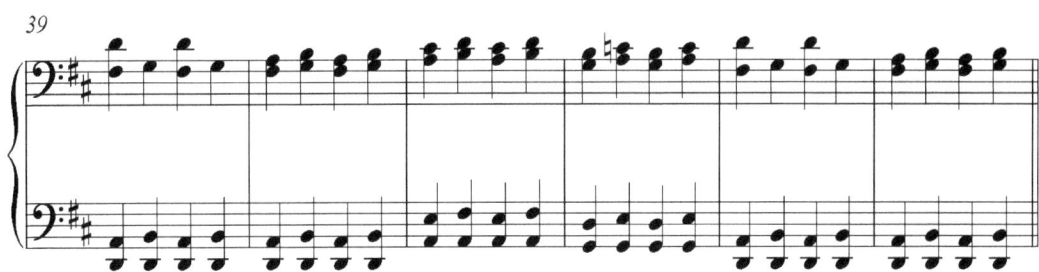

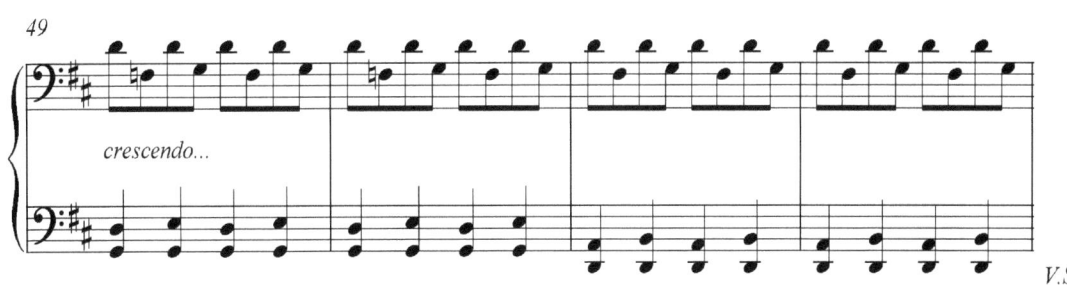

V.S

Mobile Phone Boogie: Piano page 5 of 5

Ten Jazzy, Bluesy & Funky Songs for Children

Piano page 1 of 2

The Sleepover Song

Bouncy & funky ♩ = 140

Music & Lyrics by Trixi Field

The Sleepover Song: Piano page 2 of 2

Piano page 1 of 5

Bumble Bee Calypso

Jolly ♩ = 136

Music & Lyrics by Trixi Field

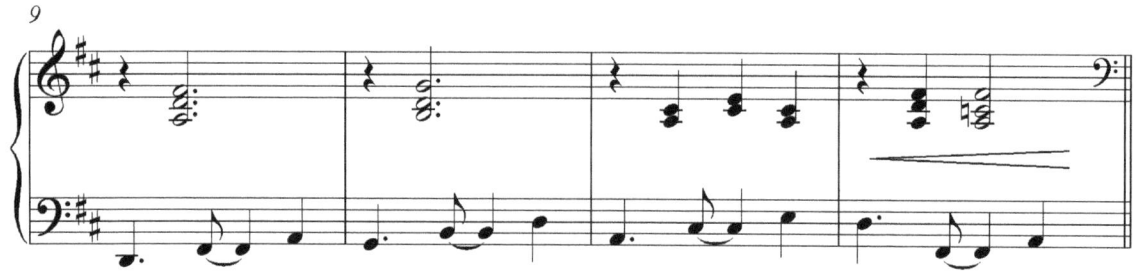

V.S.

Bumble Bee Calypso: Piano page 2 of 5

Bumble Bee Calypso: Piano page 3 of 5

Bumble Bee Calypso: Piano page 4 of 5

Bumble Bee Calypso: Piano page 5 of 5

How Can I Sing The Blues?

Music & Lyrics by Trixi Field

How Can I Sing The Blues? Piano page 2 of 4

How Can I Sing The Blues? Piano page 3 of 4

How Can I Sing The Blues? Piano page 4 of 4

Ten Jazzy, Bluesy & Funky Songs for Children

Piano page 1 of 3

Hero's Lullaby

Gently ♩ = 110

Music & Lyrics by Trixi Field

V.S.

Hero's Lullaby: Piano page 2 of 3

Hero's Lullaby: Piano page 3 of 3

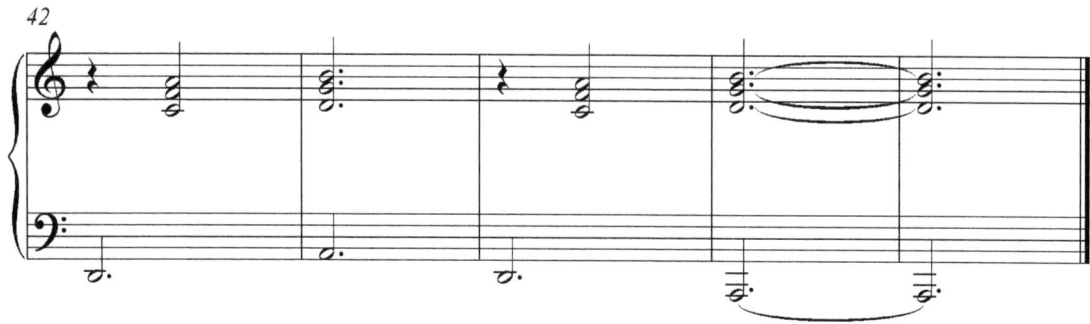

Ten Jazzy, Bluesy & Funky Songs for Children

Piano page 1 of 3

Song Train

Music & Lyrics by Trixi Field

Ten Jazzy, Bluesy & Funky Songs for Children

Piano page 1 of 3

School Uniform Blues

Jolly, with an end-of-term feel! ♩ = 140

Music & Lyrics by Trixi Field

V.S.

School Uniform Blues: Piano page 2 of 3

School Uniform Blues: Piano page 3 of 3

197

In The Hush

Music & Lyrics by Trixi Field

Gentle ♩ = 100

V.S.

Jazzicle Pops!

In The Hush: Piano page 2 of 4

V.S.

In The Hush: Piano page 3 of 4

In The Hush: Piano page 4 of 4

Ten Jazzy, Bluesy & Funky Songs for Children

Piano page 1 of 4

I Can't Get My Aeroplane To Fly

Music & Lyrics by Trixi Field

Jazzicle Pops!

I Can't Get My Aeroplane To Fly: Piano page 2 of 3

V.S.

I Can't Get My Aeroplane To Fly: Piano page 3 of 3

www.ingramcontent.com/pod-product-compliance
Ingram Content Group UK Ltd.
Pitfield, Milton Keynes, MK11 3LW, UK
UKHW051524180426
11947UKWH00018B/1568